ACTIVITY BOOK

Contents

Welcome

1 ✏️ Match and trace.

Zak   Oscar   Millie   Rita

2 ✏️🖍️ Trace. Then colour.

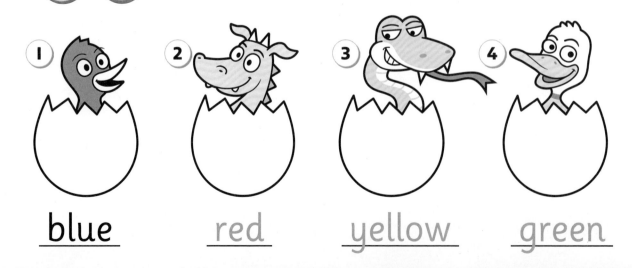

blue   red   yellow   green

3 Trace. Then count and match.

1 2 3 4 5

4 Colour and say. Then trace and match.

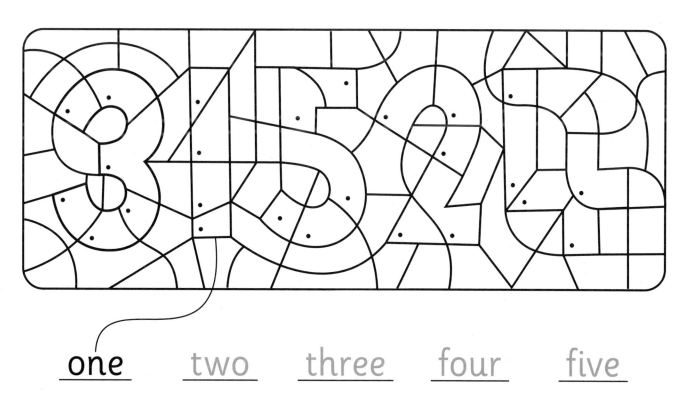

one   two   three   four   five

1 My birthday

1 ✏️✏️ **Trace and colour.**

1 pink

2 orange

3 black

4 brown

5 purple

6 white

2  Trace and match. Then say.

six   seven   eight   nine   ten

3 Join the dots.

10

9

8

2

1

3

4

7

6

5

I'm a dragon.

4  Listen and match. Then trace.

7

2

4

10

1

2

3

4

5 Read and circle.

9

I'm five / seven.

I'm three / four.

1

2

3

4

I'm six / nine.

5

8

4

I'm eight / ten.

6 🔵 1:15 ✏️ **Trace. Then listen and colour.**

b

p

7 ✏️ 💬 **Colour. Then play Bingo.**

It's blue.

◯ pink	◯ purple	◯ blue
◯ black	◯ brown	◯ _____

8 🔘 1:17 ✏️ Listen and colour.

9 ✏️ 🐸 Count and write. Then say.

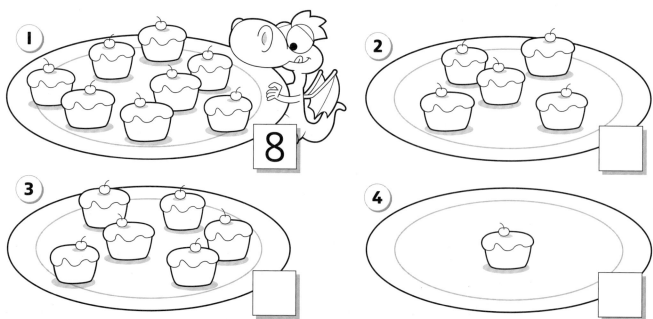

10 ✏️ Match. Then trace.

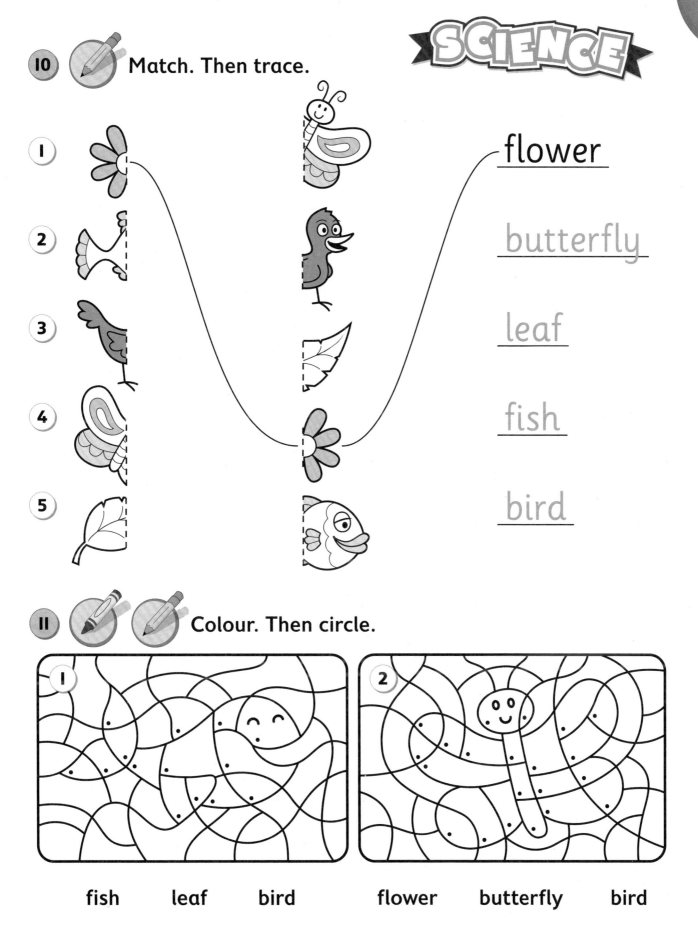

1

2

3

4

5

flower

butterfly

leaf

fish

bird

11 🖍️🖍️ Colour. Then circle.

1

2

fish   leaf   bird

flower   butterfly   bird

12 Read and colour. Then write.

It's _____.

1 It's black.

2 It's brown.

3 It's blue.

4 It's purple.

5 It's pink.

6 It's orange.

7 It's green.

13 Find and stick.

LOOK!

2 At school

1 ✏ **Draw. Then trace.**

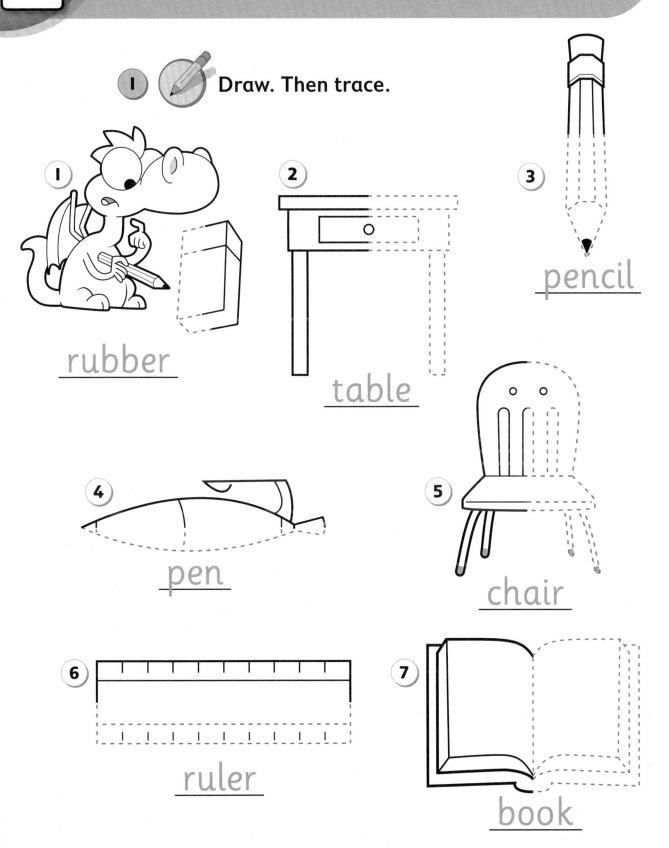

1 rubber

2 table

3 pencil

4 pen

5 chair

6 ruler

7 book

2 Find and circle.

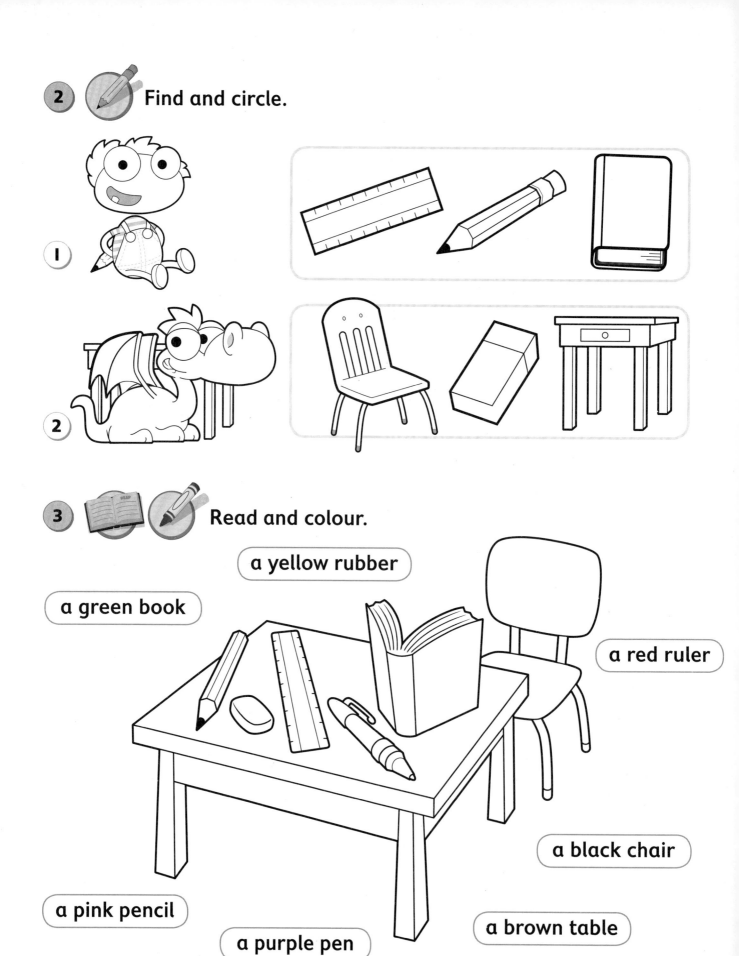

3 Read and colour.

a yellow rubber

a green book

a red ruler

a black chair

a pink pencil

a brown table

a purple pen

Listen and draw.

1.

2.

3.

4.

5.  **Find and count. Then trace and write.**

4	_rubbers_
	pencils
	rulers
	books

 **6** Trace. Then listen, match and colour.

7 Join the dots. Then trace and say.

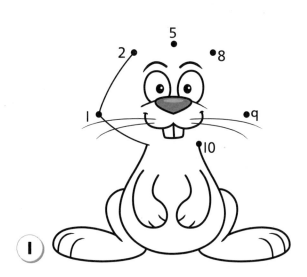

① It's a ___rabbit___ .

② It's a ___lamb___ .

8   **Listen and number.**

q   **Match and trace. Then say.**

This is my _mum_.

book　　　flower　　　chair

10 Match and trace. Then say. **MUSIC**

piano   guitar   drum   violin

11 Read and circle.

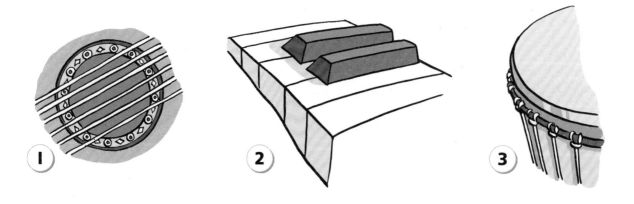

It's a (guitar) / drum.   It's a piano / violin.   It's a piano / drum.

12   **Look and write.**

pencils   pens   book   rubber   rulers   ~~table~~   chair

1

a <u>table</u>

2

a _____

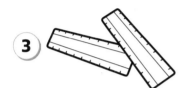

3

two _____

4

a _____

5

four _____

6

three _____

7

a _____

13  **Find and stick. Then colour.**

1 Trace. Then match.

dad   sister   brother   mum

brother   sister

This is my family.

friend

2   **Find and colour. Then circle.**

He's nine / ten.

She's seven / eight.

3 **Look and write. Then say.**

seven
~~ten~~
five
eight

1 He's __ten__ .

2 She's _____ .

3 She's _____ .

4 He's _____ .

④ 🔘 1:45 ✏️ Listen and ✔ or ✗.

⑤ ✏️ 😀💬 Trace. Then find and circle in green or blue.

He's ___happy___. 👦   She's ___sad___. 👧

6  **Trace. Then listen and match.**

7  **Count. Then write and trace.**

1

2

 seals

zebras

8 Read. Then circle.

1 This is my mum.

2 This is my friend.

3 This is my brother.

9 Find and write. Then say.

He's six.

She's eight.

She's seven.

1

2

3 6

10 1:50 ✏️ **Listen and number.**

SOCIAL SCIENCE

doctor	teacher
vet	pilot **1**

11 📖 ✏️ **Match. Then read and trace.**

1 2 3 4

She's a __vet__.   He's a __teacher__.

He's a __pilot__.   She's a __doctor__.

12 Read and write.

family
mum
friend
brother
sister
dad

This is my **family**.

1 my _____

2 my _____

3 my _____

4 my _____

5 my _____

13 Stick Find and stick.

LOOK!

4 My body

1 ✏️ Trace. Then number.

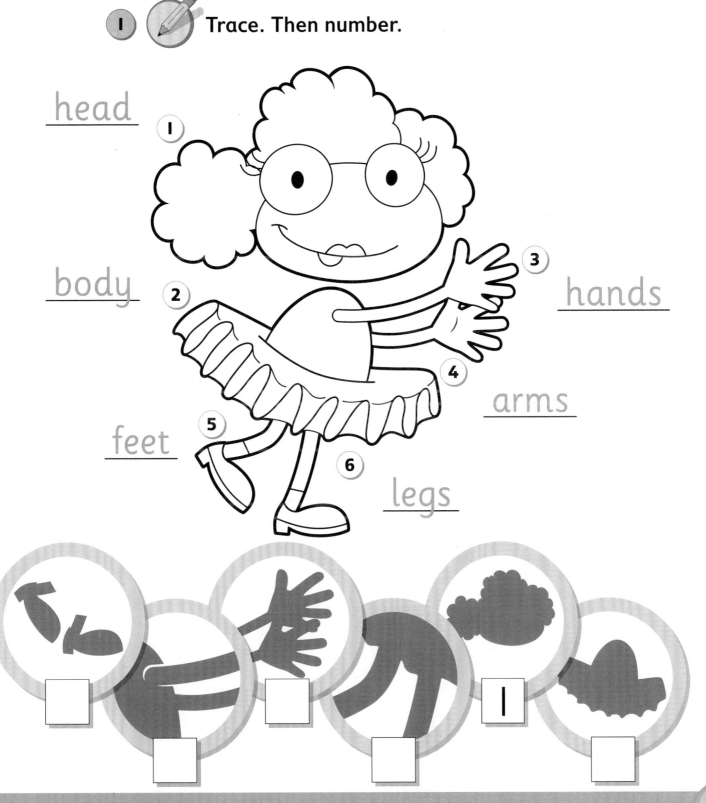

head

body

feet

hands

arms

legs

 **2** Trace. Then find and circle.

1 <u>feet</u>

2 <u>wings</u>

3 <u>tail</u>

 **3** Read and colour.

Count and trace. Then say.

I've got three legs.

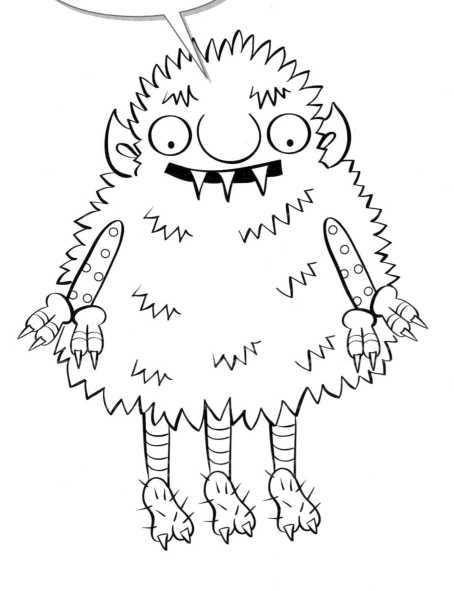

fingers

arms

3 legs

toes

feet

6  Trace. Then listen and circle.

7  Draw. Then trace and say.

① I've got a __guitar__ .

② I've got two __hands__ .

8   Listen and colour.

1

2

3

9   Draw and match. Then say.

1

2

3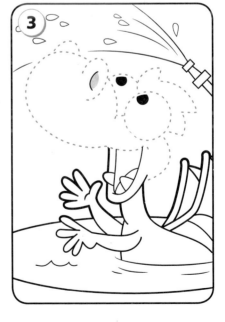

head   feet   hands

10 ✏️ Look and circle.

II 🔊 2:14 Listen and check.

30 Lesson 6

 I CAN DO IT!

12  **Draw. Then read and write.**

~~heads~~ legs toes fingers
arms feet hands

I've got two __heads__.

four _____

four _____

eight _____

three _____

three _____

six _____

LOOK!

13  **Find and stick. Then colour.**

5 My pets

 **1** Find. Then trace.

parrot

cat

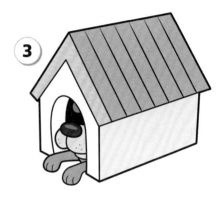

dog

frog

rabbit

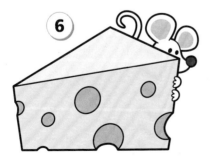

mouse

tortoise

2 Trace and match. Then say.

It's <u>big</u>.

It's <u>small</u>.

3 Find and circle the odd one out.

1

2

3

4   Listen and circle.

1

2

5  Trace. Then read and number.

1 He's got a __rabbit__. **3** He's got a __dog__.

2 She's got a __frog__. **4** She's got a __cat__.

    1

6 Trace. Then listen and ✔.

SOUNDS FUN!

7 Trace. Then circle in green or blue and say.

drum   dad   dog

two   ten   tortoise

 **8** 2:29 **Listen and number.**

q **Read and draw. Then say.**

He's got a dog.   She's got a fish.

Trace. Then match.

puppy   kitten   chick

11  **Join the dots. Then circle and say.**

1 It's a kitten / puppy / chick.   **2** It's a kitten / puppy / chick.

 **12** **Read and write.**

cat   ~~dog~~   rabbit   mouse   parrot   frog   tortoise   cat

He's got a . . .

__dog__   _____

_____   _____

She's got a . . .

_____   _____

_____   _____

13 **Stick** **Find and stick.** **LOOK!**

1 Draw. Then trace.

This is my house.

window

bedroom

door

bathroom

kitchen

living room

 **Read and match.**

He's in the bathroom.

She's in the bedroom.

She's in the kitchen.

He's in the living room.

3 **Join the dots. Then circle and say.**

He's in the bedroom / living room.

4 ✏️ **Find and count.**

in the garden ☐

in the bedroom ☐

in the bathroom ☐

5 📖 ✏️ **Read and draw.**

① It's in the _garden_ .

② It's in the _bed_ .

③ It's in the _bath_ .

6  Trace. Then listen and circle.

1

V

drum   garden   violin

2

W

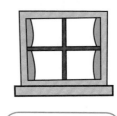
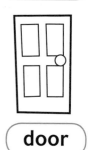

guitar   window   door

7 Find and colour in green or blue.

v = green

w = blue

8 2:45 Listen and match.

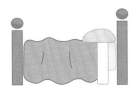   

9   Read and ✓ or ✗.

 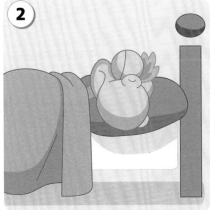 

He's in the kitchen. ✓

He's in the living room.

He's in the bathroom.

10 🖊 💿 2:47 **Trace. Then listen and draw.**

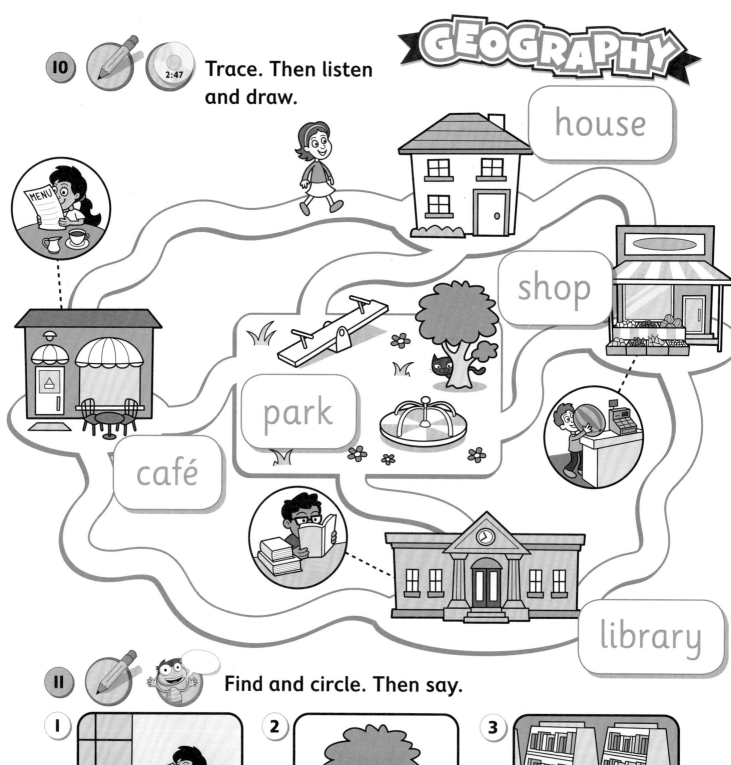

GEOGRAPHY

house

shop

park

café

library

11 🖊 😃 **Find and circle. Then say.**

1

She's in the park / café.

2

It's in the shop / park.

3

He's in the library / café.

12  Read and write.

Where's Vava?

I CAN DO IT!

bedroom   bathroom
~~kitchen~~   living room

1

He's in the **kitchen**.

2

He's in the _____.

3

He's in the _____.

4

He's in the _____.

13 Find and stick. **LOOK!**

      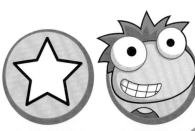

7 Food

1 🖊 Draw. Then trace.

1 meat

2 bread

3 yoghurt

4 fruit

5 cheese

6 milk

7 juice

2 ✏️ ✏️ **Find and colour. Then read and ✓.**

juice	☐
meat	☐
yoghurt	☐
cheese	☐
fruit	☐
bread	☐
milk	☐

I like . . .

3 📖 ✏️ **Read and draw.**

I like bread, fruit and cheese.

I like juice.

 **Circle the odd one out.**
Then listen and check.

1

2

  **Read and trace. Then number.**

1 I like <u>honey</u>.

2 I like <u>meat</u>.

3 I don't like <u>jelly</u>.

4 I don't like <u>cheese</u>.

6 3:10 **Trace. Then listen and play Bingo.**

SOUNDS FUN!

I like __jelly__.

I like __yoghurt__.

j   y   j

j   j   y

7 **Trace and colour.**

1 __juice__

2 __yoghurt__

3 __jelly__

4 __yellow__

8  Listen and ✓ or ✗.

STORY

9 Read and match. Then say.

I like . . .

cheese   milk

fruit   bread   fish

10 ✏ Find and trace.

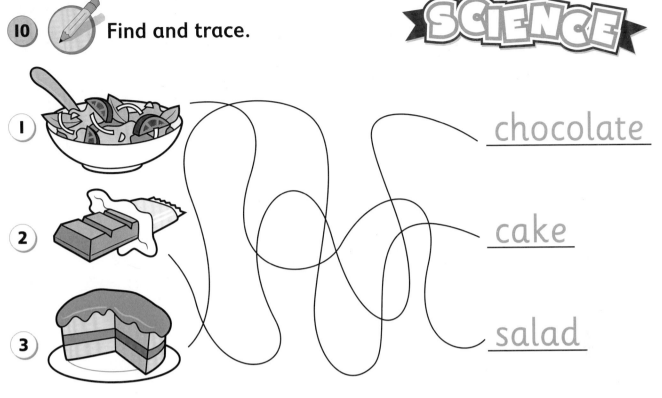

1

2

3

chocolate

cake

salad

11 📖 ✏ Read and ✓. Then draw.

It's good for me!

fruit ☐

salad ☐

cake ☐

bread ☐

yoghurt ☐

milk ☐

juice ☐

chocolate ☐

 **12** Find. Then read and write.

bread	jelly	meat	honey
yoghurt	juice	milk	

I like . . .
bread

I don't like . . .

13  Find and stick.

8 I'm excited

 Trace and number.

1 I'm ___hungry___. **2** I'm ___thirsty___. **3** I'm ___tired___.

4 I'm ___excited___. **5** I'm ___scared___.

1

2 🔘 3:22 ✏️ Listen and ✓ or ✗.

1 ✓
2 ☐
3 ☐
4 ☐

3 📖 ✏️ Find. Then read and circle.

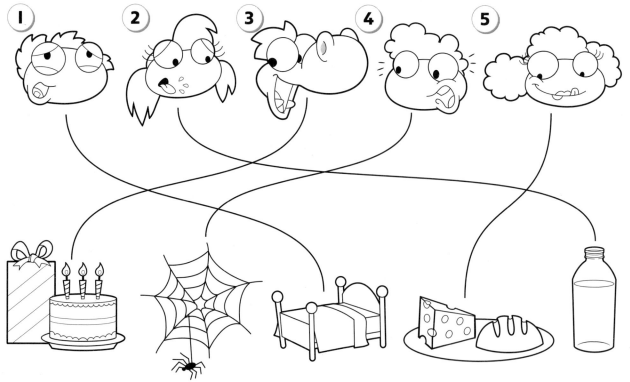

1 He's excited / (tired).

2 She's thirsty / tired.

3 He's excited / thirsty.

4 He's scared / hungry.

5 She's excited / hungry.

 **4** Match.

 stamp  jump  clap  turn around

 **5** Trace. Then circle in green or blue.

 drink eat

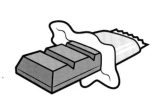  

6 Trace and colour.

SOUNDS FUN!

sh = blue

ch = green

7 3:26 Circle the odd one out. Then listen and check.

1

chocolate

shadow

chair

2

cheese

shell

shark

   Listen and number.

 **Draw and trace. Then say.**

This is my
mum.

I'm
happy.

10   **Read and ✓ or ✗.**
Then say.

1 It's a big shadow. ✓

2 It's a small shadow.

3 It's a big shadow.

11  **Read and circle.**

①

It's a table / (chair)

②

It's a hand / head.

③

It's a frog / butterfly.

④

It's a window / door.

12   **Find. Then read and write.**

| scared | excited | hungry | thirsty | ~~tired~~ |

1 He's _____tired_____.

2 He's _____.

3 She's _____.

4 She's _____.

5 He's _____.

LOOK!

13 **Stick** **Find and stick.**

Picture dictionary

Colours

red yellow green blue pink purple orange brown black white

Numbers

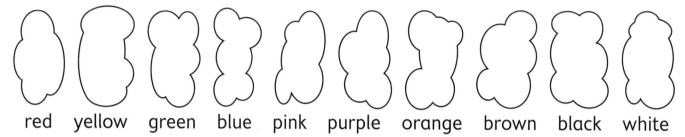

one two three four five six seven eight nine ten

Classroom objects

pen pencil book ruler rubber table chair

Family and friends

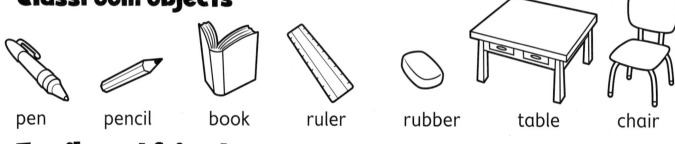

mum dad brother sister friend

My body

body head arms hands fingers legs feet toes

Animals

| dog | cat | rabbit | parrot | mouse | tortoise | frog |

In the house

| house | garden | kitchen | living room |

| bedroom | bathroom | door | window |

Food and drink

| meat | fruit | bread | cheese | yoghurt | milk | juice |

Feelings

| happy | sad | excited | scared | tired | hungry | thirsty |

Halloween

1 🖊️ Match. Then trace.

① ② ③ ④ ⑤

witch   pumpkin   cat   monster   bat

2 🖊️ Join the dots. Then circle.

I'm a monster / pumpkin / witch.

Christmas

1 3:38 **Trace and match. Then listen and colour.**

sleigh   present   reindeer   Santa

2 **Draw and say. Then write and trace.**

To _____
Happy
Christmas!
From Santa.

Easter

1 Trace. Then colour and write.

 bunny   chick    egg

It's an _____.

2  Look and draw.

1   

2      

3